NONPROFIT FUNDRAISING

HACKS

Practical Psychological Tactics & Strategies

By Salvador Briggman

Table of Contents

Introduction

In my last book, Nonprofit Crowdfunding Explained, I went over the nuts and bolts of how to run an online crowdfunding or peer to peer fundraising campaign. I showed you how to go from having absolutely no web presence to attracting donors, getting media attention, and hitting an ambitious fundraising goal. This book, Nonprofit Fundraising Hacks, is the handy marketing toolbox that you can reference for practical tactics and teachings. It will reveal the psychological tricks that you can use to raise more money from your existing donors (or new ones).

Think of this as the slim volume that's chocked full of pure fundraising wisdom. It forms the foundation of a seemingly magical system for turning cold stone strangers into raving supporters. Many of the strategies I'll be introducing are so easy to learn and so effective that you'll be scratching your head, wondering why you haven't been using them all along! Rather than going through the painstaking process of figuring out all these tricks yourself, I'll deliver them to you in this easy-to-digest guide.

I have to be honest with you though. Having been an online marketer for eight years, I've come into contact with these principles many times. In fact, I'd go so far as to say that *most* successful nonprofits and established companies use these tactics. It's because they're proven to work to raise more funds. However, they *aren't* introduced to the millions of nonprofits throughout the world. You have to operate in the dark and you're left wondering how to make ends meet at the end of the month. That's not fair!

Hopefully, this book will help to level the playing field, so that you can compete with some of the bigger organizations out there in the nonprofit industry. You'll discover science-backed ways to get more funding for your nonprofit. These are breakthrough marketing strategies that are easy to implement and just plain work. Mark my words, some of them will boggle your mind. When you begin to act on the advice, you'll start to see results that not only affect your bottom line, but also give you the power to *help more people*.

At the end of the day, that's all that matters, isn't it?

The people you're helping. The way you're impacting the world for the positive. This fundraising guff isn't all that fun or exciting. What's more, you spend so much of your time doing it. That's why I wanted to put together a paint by numbers formula for handling this area of your operations, once and for all. Once you harness this linchpin skill, you won't ever have to worry about how you'll pay next month's bills. Instead of struggling to stay afloat, you'll have a rock-solid fundraising plan in place, and be able to live an empowered life.

If you're fed up with seeing the big-boys cash in on fundraising, and annoyed that there isn't better training out there for nonprofit leaders, like you, then this is the book for you. I want to bring some of these effective for-profit marketing techniques to the nonprofit world so that you can impact more people at a fraction of the cost. As you know, that's the name of the game. The more you know, the easier it will be for you to navigate this changing terrain.

Let's get started!

- **Salvador Briggman**

Chapter 1:

The Online Giving Revolution

Right now, we're in the middle of an online giving revolution. The rules of the game are changing fast. Where once you could rely on the tried and true methods of physical mailers and automated phone calls, now you must use new methods to engage potential donors. If you don't, you risk missing out on the greatest gift since the invention of the computer.

In the next few chapters, we'll be dialing in on how to raise more money online using scientifically backed findings. Before we get there, I want to give you crystal clear picture of the landscape we're now in so that you can navigate the terrain with the right map. This will help you to grasp the importance of what I'll be sharing in this book, and why implementing some of the techniques that I'll reveal will have a near-immediate effect on your fundraising efforts.

In 2014, Blackbaud surveyed 3,000+ nonprofit organizations and released a study on charitable giving. The report showed that overall, charitable giving revenue grew by 4.9% in 2013. Sounds respectable, right?

However, compared to 2012, *online giving* grew by 13.5%, with the largest amount of growth happening in small nonprofits to the tune of 18.4%. This is the second year that online giving has shown a double-digit growth rate. Although online giving only accounted for 6.4% of all charitable giving in 2013, it is the fastest growing sector, particularly among faith-based organizations and smaller nonprofits. As of 2018, it accounts for 8.5% of overall fundraising, according to the Charitable Giving Report.

What does this mean? Even though tried and true methods of fundraising work and brought in over $10 billion dollars for nonprofits in this study, the power of the internet, smartphones, and an increasingly social media savvy donor base is changing the fundraising game, and you need to take notice.

The Rate of Smartphone Adoption

You'd be hard-pressed to find an inventor in 1900 that would have predicted that even a child could hold all of the world's cumulative knowledge in the palm of their hand by the first decade of the 21st Century. But, that's exactly what a smartphone is: a miniature computer that lets you stay connected 24/7, whether you're at home or on the go.

More and more, millennials and young working professionals are no longer turning to their computer, the radio, or even the TV for entertainment. They're checking their Facebook feed from their phone, going on Snapchat, browsing Instagram, or reading up on the latest news on Twitter. A person's attention, the most sought-after commodity, is more difficult to maintain than ever before.

According to Nielsen's 2013 study, the smartphone penetration rate has reached 64 percent in the United States, with 80 percent of new buyers choosing a smartphone as their mobile handset device. This estimate is backed up by the Pew Research Center, which pegged smartphone adoption at 56% of the American adult population in 2013. However, since then, there have been claims that the US has reached a "smartphone saturation" point and is now seeing a rate of 75% smartphone penetration.

In fact, smartphone adoption is on the rise all over the world. eMarketer recently released a study citing that the number of smartphones worldwide will surpass 2 billion in 2016, which is in line with Business Insider's report that nearly 22% of the world population owned a smartphone in 2013.

Yes, this means that your son or daughter now can play games all the time, have two-way video calls with their friends, and easily capture the moments that matter to them, with interesting photo filters or captions. But, it also that the way in which we receive, spread, and process news has fundamentally shifted as a society.

The Rise of The Social Web

Arguably, the worldwide web has had three major phases. The first being an information consumption phase. During this time, you could check out your friend's nonprofit website, which was mainly static, get information and click around a few links. It functioned as a glorified brochure that was a small complimentary feature to getting a real brochure in the mail, watching video tapes, seeing TV ads, or calling up the actual office.

Next, we began to see the rise of search engines, bloggers, and online transactions. Search engines, particularly Google, made it easy to connect with organizations that you cared about or to learn more about particular causes. You might forward an email to your friend, receive an email chain letter, or comment on a particular news story. In addition, you might have read or run a personal online blog, which has other readers and has opinions on ongoing events. In fact, as of 2014, 6.7 million people actively blog and 77% of internet users read blogs.

Although online transactions have always been met with a bit of skepticism, everyday internet users were beginning to become accustomed to the idea of purchasing items online, which may have been recommended by a blogger, or that they found while searching on Google.

We've entered the day of the social web, where smartphones, online video, high quality websites, and social networks like Facebook, Twitter, and YouTube are changing up the fundraising game. Now, an individual doesn't need a blog, website, or even YouTube channel to share the stories and causes that they care about. They can do it with the click of a button from their Facebook account.

According to Digital Insights, as of 2014, Facebook has over 1 billion monthly active mobile users, which is comprised of 75% of adults. In addition, over 500 million tweets are sent per day with 78% active on mobile devices. Although a newer social network, Instagram already has over 200 million monthly active users and 20+ Billion photos have been shared on Instagram to date. Finally, the video viewing and sharing network YouTube, which was founded in 2005, has already amassed over 1 billion users, with 40% of YouTube traffic coming from mobile.

As one of the newer social networks, Instagram has only been around since 2010, but represents the beginning of a new trend towards the socialization of the mobile device. In fact, SnapChat, which was founded in 2011, has reported that users send 700 million photos per day and that Snapchat Stores are viewed 500 million times per day, now with the addition of notable networks like CNN, the Food Network, National Geographic, Yahoo News, and more.

A tidal wave is beginning to form that will change online giving and donor relations as we know it. The question is not if it's going to happen. The question is how will you respond. Will you surf on the top of the new wave or be drawn beneath its depths?

The Success of The ALS Ice Bucket Challenge

In 2014, the world witnessed the success of "The ALS Ice Bucket Challenge," which ended up raising $100 million dollars for the ALS Association, which helps bring awareness to and advocate for patients that have suffered from issues related to amyotrophic lateral sclerosis (ALS), also known as Lou Gehrig's disease.

The challenge, which turned overnight into a worldwide sensation, was simple. As a Facebook user, you might be nominated by a friend or acquaintance to participate in the ALS Ice Bucket Challenge. Within 24 hours of being nominated, you could either donate $100 to help combat ALS or video tape yourself pouring a bucket of ice water on your head. In many cases, high net worth individuals chose to do both. After participating in the challenge, you would have the chance to nominate up to three other participants who would then need to complete the challenge within 24 hours.

These simple rules and the time-sensitive nature of the challenge turned a small effort to help raise awareness for ALS into a growing snowball. By the end of social media tsunami, there were 2.4 million tagged videos circulating

Facebook. Celebrities including Bill Gates, Barak Omaba, George W. Bush, Matt Damon, LeBron James, and more had participated in the movement.

Although there have been criticisms that the challenge focused more on "having fun" than cultivating the habit of lifelong charitable contribution, it's clear that social media and the internet has completely transformed nonprofit giving behaviors. While once brochures, physical mail, and personal phone calls were sworn by as effective methods to stay in touch with and engage donors. They are now being replaced by other information channels.

Don't get me wrong. Engaging in direct marketing and outreach is still important. However, when the conversation and communication channels change from one platform to another, you must go where the crowd is to stay relevant in this loud and competitive world. Otherwise, you might find yourself getting left behind.

Online Giving Grew By 12.1% in 2017

According to **Nonprofitssource**, when it comes to 2017, *$31 billion* was raised through online giving. There are a few important key facts I want to note:

- *Giving Tuesday* raised $274 million dollars online

- $128 is the average *online donation* amount.

- $326 dollars is the average *annual donation* total for recurring donors.

- Only *67%* of nonprofits across the globe are *set up to accept online donations.*

- The average nonprofit crowdfunding campaign raises *$9,237.55*

- 21% of donations are directly through *social media.*

- *Email messaging* drove 28% of all online fundraising revenue

- 25% of donors complete their donations on *mobile devices*

"Trends in the 2017 Charitable Giving Report show very positive signs for the emergence of digital and mobile giving," said Steve MacLaughlin, vice president of data and analytics at Blackbaud and senior advisor to the Blackbaud Institute.

30% of Online Giving Occurs in December

… and 10% in the last three days of the year. Woah!

This is according to Network For Good and their stats, citing that the average gift size is $236. In 2017, nonprofits raised 7.6% of their total fundraising revenue online, and 13.9% for smaller nonprofits. This is according to the 2017 Blackbaud Charitable Giving Report.

As you read these statistics you should be thinking… so… online giving is *seasonal.*

If you're a traditional nonprofit organization and are just now venturing into the online giving arena, then it might make sense to concentrate most of your efforts on a #GivingTuesday campaign or a fundraiser throughout the month of December.

This could also be true of launching a peer to peer fundraising or crowdfunding campaign. It might pay to wait until one of these months, where your existing donors will be most likely to give to the initiative.

85% of Volunteers Donated to their Nonprofit

Charitable giving isn't just about wanting to help. It's also about wanting to see that your help is *effective.*

Your hardcore donors must believe in the mission of the nonprofit, believe that your work produces results, and care or empathize with the demographic you're helping.

The easiest way to accomplish these three tasks is to get them to volunteer with your charity. It gives them a first-hand experience of the kind of work you're up to and, what's more, makes it more likely they will become annual donors.

In 2018, 66% of donors volunteered within the last 12 months and 85% of them donated to the nonprofit that they volunteered for.

A successfully nonprofit fundraising strategy is not only about using these new mediums, like online giving, but also *engaging* members of the community in your nonprofit's work. Ironically, this will help you raise more money over time!

29% of Donors Say Social Media Gets Them To Give

One of the critical findings in the 2018 giving report is that 29% of donors say that social media inspires them to give to charities and nonprofits.

As you can see, most of the communications that inspire giving happen online, including social media, email, and a nonprofit's websites.

If you're running a nonprofit organization, then you can't afford to NOT be online. Think of Facebook as your own personal TV channel where you can post videos, images, and even communicate with your donors. The same goes for other social networks.

Social media is the primary way that users find out about what their friends are up to, cool new events they can attend, neat products to buy, and of course, new causes they should support.

TV and Radio Inspire Only 9% of Donors to Give

If I had a tv-soundtrack for "crickets," then I'd play it right now.

TV is *DEAD.* People are cutting the cord in greater numbers and almost everyone is tuning out of advertisements.

The funny thing is that when an advertisement comes on, you pick up your phone and start to browse Facebook, Twitter, YouTube, or Instagram.

Think about that... existing TV viewers are taking their attention during the commercials and directing it towards social media. You should be "advertising" on social media, not on TV.

I think it's clear that:

- Netflix and YouTube have replaced TV

- Blogs have replaced newspapers

- Podcasts have replaced radio

- Online giving is beginning to *replace* traditional giving

It's only a matter of time folks. You can either step up and take advantage of this new opportunity or continue to struggle with the old methods, which are quickly proving to be outdated and ineffective.

So, What Gets Donors to Give?

In my last book, <u>Nonprofit Crowdfunding Explained</u>, I shared with you a step-by-step strategy for raising money from the crowd. We went into exactly what you gotta do to launch a killer crowdfunding or peer to peer fundraising campaign. This book is now available on <u>Amazon</u> and <u>Audible.</u>

After I wrote this book, I became *saddened.*

I felt like I was leaving out SO MANY nonprofits that can use online fundraising to bring extra fundraising revenue into their organization.

The problem is that nonprofits are not used to the "marketing" skills and "technology" know-how that comes easy to the for-profit marketplace.

I want to share with you the *key psychological triggers* that get someone to actually give you cash and donate to your cause. These are the secrets that marketers (like me) use to build up a raving fanbase and get people to take action.

By the end of this book, you'll know exactly how to turn a casual website visitor into a committed nonprofit donor.

You'll discover all the little-known ways to get them invested in your cause, excited about your vision, and eager to help with their time and money. These are powerful weapons of influence that you're about to unlock. All you have to do is keep reading.

Chapter 2:

The Science Behind Online Giving

What if I told you that there was a *scientific way* to get people interested in your nonprofit?

Well… not only interested, but actually *give money* to your cause.

As the psychology field has progressed, so too has the technology that researchers use to better understand the brain.

More and more, researchers are using functional magnetic resonance imaging or fMRI to detect changes associated with blood-flow in the brain. You can actually see which areas "light up" when you're performing certain tasks or when you're exposed to external stimuli.

Researchers can also now use blood samples to detect the presence of steroids like cortisol or oxytocin, which are associated with a particular group of emotions. These hormones work in conjunction with your brain to regulate your mood. They affect the emotions you feel on a day-to-day basis.

Before we get into some of the fundraising hacks that you can use in your own marketing and outreach efforts, I want to share a study conducted by Dr. Paul Zak, a scientist and author. Dr. Zak is the founding Director of the Center for Neuroeconomics Studies and Professor of Economics, Psychology and Management at Claremont Graduate University. The scientific study he conducted actually measures the type of story that elicits hormones that are associated charitable giving.

In this psychological study, a group of researchers exposed participants to two different video-based stories with the same two characters. The researchers measured variables like hormones released in the bloodstream, heart rate, skin conductance, and respiration to see how the stories emotionally affected the participants. After watching the story, the participants were then asked whether or not they wanted to donate money to a particular cause.

The findings of this psychological study will help clue you into the emotions that you need to stimulate if you want to be virtually guaranteed of getting a person to donate to your nonprofit. For us to understand the emotions that are associated with giving, we first have to analyze the stories that were told to the group of research participants.

In the first story, there is a little boy named Ben who has brain cancer. He's been through chemo and radiation treatment, but he feels happy. He enjoys playing with his toys.

At the same time, his father is sad because even though Ben is happy, his father knows that Ben is going to die in 3 to 6 months. His father still tries to be happy around Ben, but it is difficult with this knowledge.

Towards the end of the story, Ben's father remarks how amazing it is to know how little time you have left. It makes each second that he spends with his son more precious. At this moment, the father has merged himself with Ben and feels what Ben should be feeling. It is as if the father himself is dying and slowly coming to terms with it.

After watching the story, the experimenters took blood samples from the participants to measure the hormones that were released throughout the experience. This story caused the feelings of distress and empathy. The body produced the stress hormone cortisol, which is responsible for focusing our attention on something important. It also correlates with feeling of distress. The body also produced oxytocin, which is associated with feelings of care, connection, and love. This hormone correlates with feelings of empathy.

When the participants had finished watching the first story, the experimenters then gave them a chance to share money with a stranger in the lab, or a charity that works with ill kids. They found that those participants that released **both** cortisol and oxytocin were far more likely to give money. In fact, the amount of oxytocin released predicted how much money would be shared. It's pretty clear that this story emotionally affected the participants, which opened them up to giving money to another person or charity.

This initial story was contrasted with a "control story" that basically described the very basic daily life of Ben and his father. The control story was designed to be bland and devoid of any kind of context relating to his illness. While watching this version of the story, participants did not experience any major emotions like stress or empathy. They were simply bored and waited for the video to finish. After watching this version of the story, the vast majority did not give money when asked by the experimenters.

This fascinating experiment then took a wild turn. With more funding, the researchers went back to the drawing board and asked the question… *can you predict whether or not someone will give money?*

They beefed up the study and started to measure other variables using fMRI technology to see which regions in the brain were most active during the emotional story compared to the boring story. This allowed the researchers to accurately pinpoint when someone was feeling distressed and when someone was feeling empathetic.

During the boring version of the story, participants didn't attend to the information and they blanked out. Their brain didn't light up much. Nothing was happening that was exciting or causing distress. There was no story structure.

When watching the compelling version of the story, the participants' brains lit up like crazy. The experimenters found that the most active areas during the emotional version of the story were associated with what's called "theory of the mind" or understanding what others are doing, and areas that were rich oxytocin centers.

Using this method, the researchers could predict with *80% accuracy* which study participants who saw the video would be willing to donate money to charity.

Stories transport us into other people's worlds. They allow us to feel what other people are feeling. They cause us to feel REAL emotions, like distress or empathy. These stories change our brain chemistry and our choices, thoughts, and behaviors.

In this experiment, people donated money because they wanted to help Ben and his father (or people like them). They felt a sense of how difficult it must be for these people, and by giving money, they could help alleviate those negative feelings.

In order to get someone to give money, science is telling you that you have to wrap the ask inside a story that is emotionally compelling and allows potential donors to empathize with your target demographic. If you FAIL to do this, then you will fail to elicit those feelings of *distress* and *empathy* that highly correlate with giving behavior.

While you might not think of raising money as "sales," it is a battle of persuasion. You basically have to convince someone else that giving money is in their best interest. According to the social science of economics, we all only behave and make decisions based on our self-interest. So, how do you appeal to someone's interest to get them to give?

It's all about emotions. As human beings, our brains are filled up with two things: thoughts and feelings. We're either thinking about how to solve problems, or wrapped up in our feelings about the world, things that are happening, and life in general.

In fact, we actually enjoy our emotions so much that we will go to big movie theaters just to sit there for two hours and feel different emotions. You gotta appeal to a human's emotions if you want to get them to buy a product or give money.

In the past, a nonprofit might have to go door to door to solicit donations. They'd have to send out physical mailers to get on someone's radar. Now a days, anyone can have the power of an entire TV network simply through their social media channels.

A nonprofit can create a video that racks up hundreds of thousands of views on social media, leading to a surge of donations to their cause. This means that you now have all of the tools that you need to kindle the emotions that lead to online giving. Honestly, what's stopping you?

Not only that, but you can use the internet to build up an email list of people who actually want to receive information from you. That's powerful!

This email list can be responsible for a burst of traffic on a campaign page. It can lead to a flurry of donations when you launch a new initiative. All of these tools are available to you, but you must also use them effectively if you want to raise funds. You gotta know how to trigger emotions that lead to giving.

You must first FEEL something before you give money to an online fundraising campaign. You then justify that decision with logic. All too often, nonprofits will rattle off statistics or boring bits of information that don't serve to get someone excited and bought-in to their vision. They then wonder why no one is giving money!

In the next few chapters, I'll share with you exactly how to get donors to commit using proven marketing techniques.

For now, I want to explore a complete list of the emotions that lead to online giving.

Emotion #1: Empathy

When it comes to our focus and life perspective, there are three core states we can be in.

1. Focused on *our own* emotions, thoughts, and goals. Often times, we feel a bit selfish when doing this, but it's necessary. Someone who does this to the extreme is described as narcissistic or self-centered.

2. Focus on *someone else's* emotions, thoughts, and goals. We feel what they feel, and to a certain degree, we momentarily lose our "sense of self."

3. Focused on the situation. Rationally observing the situation that's unfolding like a scientist. This is a *problem-solving mode.*

Empathy refers to the second mental state, where we FEEL what someone else is feeling. We then want to do something to alleviate their pain (because it gives us pain) or celebrate their joy, because we take pleasure in seeing them happy.

Love and empathy are closely tied together. When we love someone, we care about their wellbeing without thinking about our own. We momentarily lose a sense of self.

Someone who donates money to a charity feels a HIGH DEGREE of empathy with either the person asking them for the donation or the target demographic the nonprofit is helping.

Emotion #2: Rapport

Rapport is very closely tied to empathy, but it's actually a precursor. To feel empathy with someone, you must first be in rapport with them.

You tend FEEL in rapport with someone when you agree with their beliefs, lifestyle, ideas, and likely have a similar world view. Some indicators include:

- Similar world view and values

- Same social class or upbringing

- Part of the same tribe or group

- Both have the same aspirations, hobbies, etc.

Going back to Kindergarten, if you want to make friends, you want to be as similar as possible to the people you're trying to bond with. You don't want to accentuate your differences.

These similarities could even be as simple as gender. For example, if a mother sees a mother bear defending and her cub from predators, that person feels a certain degree of kinship with them.

It sounds silly, but if that person was a bear, they'd do the same in that situation. Similarities develop rapport and rapport enhances our feelings of empathy with others.

Emotion #3: Alleviate Pain or Feel Joy

Once you have developed rapport and empathy with someone, they will FEEL pain if you are hurt. You can even watch a video of a complete stranger falling down and wince.

"Ouch… that's gotta hurt."

Great fundraising pages will accentuate this unsettling feeling until the potential donor says "I can't stand it. I'm going to donate. At least then I'll be helping."

This is the real reason why you see those horrible television fundraising commercials that prey on any human being's emotions. They showcase children with swollen bellies or dogs that have been discarded.

Know what I mean?

Yeah... it sucks. Any normal person seeing a child in pain would want to help.

If done correctly, you can focus a person's mind on the pain experienced by the target demographic in order to get them to help out.

Keep in mind that done in the wrong way, this can be extremely manipulative. But, if done for a good cause and in the right way, it can be very effective. The same can be true for positive emotions.

Most of us like seeing when someone is truly happy. Especially if they have a wildly genuine happy reaction.

I'm sure that you've seen videos that have been passed around on Facebook, like the one where an older man is gushing over a beautiful rainbow.

We can't help but smile!

Knowing that a donation will help someone else's life in a large will make us feel joy. It's one of the core reasons that people donate online.

Emotion #4: Positive Expectancy and Trust

It's very rare that someone will give money to a nonprofit selflessly.

They want to see change happen. They're giving money to make a difference.

According to the CEO of Achieve and researcher for The Millennial Impact Derrick Feldmann, "What motivates millennials is a desire to affect THEIR cause through YOUR organization with their friends."

This is also true of older generations. Now a days, with only a small fraction of a donation going towards helping the in-need demographic, the public is more skeptical than ever before.

For some charities and nonprofits, anywhere from 50 – 80% of their fundraising dollars go towards overhead costs. NOT the actual people that they were designed to help.

That's insane!

Would you give $100 if you knew that $85 of it was paying someone's salary and only $15 was helping out the individuals in need? I don't think so.

You must PROVE to potential donors that their money is actually going to help people. This allows them to expect that something positive will come from the action of giving.

The only reason why a donor believes your claims is because you've built up trust and credibility. This is the foundation from which a donation is made.

Without trust, money is not changing hands.

Emotion #5: Anger or Disgust

When we see injustice in the world, we get angry.

The same can be said of any event that violates how we believe the world should work.

For example, in 2012, a video surfaced online where a bus monitor named Karen Klein was bullied by local kids. They hurled profanity, insults, and threats her way.

One even said, "you don't have a family because they all killed themselves because they don't want to be near you." Klein's oldest son killed himself 10 year ago.

This video was shared all over the web and people were:

- Outraged

- Disgusted

- Ashamed

It made people feel like an injustice had happened and it had to be righted in some way. An Indiegogo campaign was launched for her and she ended raising $703,168!

These emotions directly led to donations. By giving money, people felt a little bit better and that they had "at least done something" to combat the wickedness.

Emotion #6: Identity and Obligation

The next reason why people give money in person and online comes down to the feeling of identity consistency and obligation. Let me explain.

When you commit to a belief, cause, or decision (even in a small way), you will feel a sense of cognitive dissonance if you do something that conflicts with that commitment. You'll feel anxious, nervous, and inauthentic. This will cause you to comply with your original commitment.

For example, if someone comes up to you and asks you these questions:

1. Do you believe you are a good person?

2. Do you believe in supporting the environment?

3. Have you contributed to supporting this in the past?

And then asks you to support a charity initiative, then you'll be far more likely to comply with that request. Why?

Because you've already painted yourself as a upstanding charitable member of society. To act in a way that is inconsistent with that image would hurt your ego and sense of identity. It would feel… awkward. You'd feel guilty.

You might try to find a reason NOT to comply with that request, but if you're unable to, then you most likely will, even if it's only for $5. Giving money feels better than the guilt you'd feel if you didn't.

Yes – this is a tad bit manipulative, but it can be used in less invasive ways to encourage potential donors to become advocates.

Along with this idea of consistency, there is also the feeling of obligation that can cause you to give money to charity. That feeling might come out of your sense of identity, previously stated beliefs, or because a charity has helped you or someone you know in some way.

For example, if someone came up to you (like the hare krishna group) and gave you a flower. You'd smile and thank them. Then, if they asked for a $5 donation, you'd likely comply. You wouldn't want to, but you'd feel guilty and awkward about it.

You might try to give the flower back, but if they wouldn't accept it, you'd still feel negative. The only way to stop feeling negative would be to donate money or stomp away and try to forget the encounter.

Now, I also believe this is a tad bit manipulative, but gifts and free value can be used to engender trust and warm people up to giving to your nonprofit.

Emotion #7: Significance and Meaning

Finally, the core reason that someone will give money or donate to a nonprofit is because they want to feel significant and that their life has meaning.

By donating to a cause, that person is having a real change in the world. Their life has purpose. They are making other people's lives better. They also feel significant when you thank them profusely for the donation.

In order to make someone feel this way, you must take specific actions like:

- Show them tangibly how their donation will impact others

- Thank them and be grateful, to allow them to feel significant

- Treat them as special members of your community

We all crave to feel significant and that our life has meaning. As a nonprofit, you have the opportunity to make your donors feel this way!

Chapter 3:

Mastering Donor Psychology

I've been thinking about my online business career, and I think that you can sum up my overarching mission in one sentence. My goal is to get people to take *action*.

There's a term in the marketing world called "vanity metrics." These are metrics that simply don't matter in the long run, but that will boost your ego in the short run. This could include things like the number of visitors to your website, the number of times your message has been shared on social media, or glowing emails from people who say that they love the mission of your nonprofit.

While these things might make you feel good, they are complete bull****. At the end of the day, the only thing that matters is whether or not you've gotten donations for your fundraising campaign. Have people actually taken out their credit card and donated money?

In this chapter, I'm going to be revealing several key psychological techniques that can be used to get visitors to take action. These are the same strategies that master marketers use to sell billions of dollars-worth of product a year to consumers around the world.

Rule #1: Social Proof Creates Trust and Lowers Defensive Barriers

I'm a pretty normal young man living in NYC. I don't smell, I'm reasonably intelligent, and I'm told I have a nice smile.

But, if I were to go up to a random person on the street and say "Hi, nice day, right?" more often than not, I'd get looks of confusion, suspicion, annoyance, and many people would nervously smile and rush past.

I know this because I actually do this sometimes just to work on my social skills and face social fear.

People are naturally suspicious in our culture of strangers and organizations that we haven't heard of before. It's because the person *suspects* that the other person wants something from them, which puts them on the defensive and raises their guard.

There is no familiarity, trust, or value in the interaction. Also, everyone else is on their way to work or another destination, so it feels "weird" for them to respond to or stop and talk to a complete stranger. It's an interruption.

Social proof is one way to jump this barrier and gain instant trust. Here's how Wikipedia defines it:

"Social proof, also known as informational social influence, is a psychological phenomenon where people assume the actions of others in an attempt to reflect correct behavior for a given situation. This effect is prominent in ambiguous social situations where people are unable to determine the appropriate mode of behavior, and is driven by the assumption that surrounding people possess more knowledge about the situation."

When a product or individual has social proof, others will approach them from a perspective of *curiosity* rather than skepticism.

They're more likely to take a second to watch your video or read your fundraising page because "other people think it's interesting, so I might as well check it out."

It's basically thinking that just because a book is bestselling that it's probably good and worth buying. You might even take less time to check it out than a non-bestselling book.

If you've ever seen a bunch of people surrounding one person in a group setting, I'm willing to bet you thought, "Is that a celebrity?" or you were more apt to go and join the crowd yourself to see who they were.

When you lead with social proof, rather than being skeptical, the prospective donor is more likely to focus on the mission, story, or awesome impact that your organization has had. They'll be curious instead of suspicious.

There are a few ways to create social proof, including:

- Testimonials

- Genuine activity and donations

- Comments section

- Media hits/write-ups

- Social sharing

- Reviews/emails

- Credentials and endorsements

While increasing the vanity metrics that we discussed earlier shouldn't be your main goal, they can be leveraged to grow your social proof or credibility in the minds of new or existing donors.

Increasing the social proof of your organization or your crowdfunding campaign is one way to get visitors to take action. A campaign with high social proof is more likely to convert browsers into donors. Rather than clicking off your page, a donor is going to open their wallet and put in their credit card information.

The worst thing that could happen is that a visitor comes to your campaign and sees 0 donations, 0 social shares, and a half-baked "ask." It makes them feel like little real work went into putting together the fundraising page. They'll rationalize that either the organization isn't serious, that the cause isn't worthy of their funds, or that something else is wrong, because no one else has given money.

On the flip side, if someone discovers your campaign online and sees a bunch of donations pouring in or massive engagement and social sharing activity, they're more likely to take a sec to watch your video and read through your pitch. The fact that other people are paying attention to the fundraising effort makes them want to learn more. It evokes curiosity and engenders a stronger feeling of trust. We're going to revisit this topic when we talk about marketing your nonprofit's online fundraising campaign.

Rule #2: A Sense of Urgency is What Prompts Action

The reason that people *take action* is because there's an impending deadline or other event, which creates a sense of urgency.

I don't know about you, but I was definitely one of those kids who procrastinated most of the college semester and then crammed two days before the exam. Many of my nights were spent in the library the day before a final paper was due.

Of course, the best and most *rational* thing to do is to plan, take action according to your plan, and see the desired result. But, most people aren't rational. We're guided by our emotions.

When someone feels a sense of urgency about a particular activity, they will:

- Focus and drone out distractions.

- Take massive action in a small amount of time.

- Overcome hurdles that would normally set them back.

- Pay less attention to hindering emotions or thoughts.

- Look to short-cut signals to make micro decisions.

- Take more risks.

I've written and spoken extensively about how a nonprofit's fundraising meter will grow and flatten out over time. Many campaigners see an influx of donations towards the beginning and end of their campaign. Both of these events create a sense of urgency among supporters, whether it's to claim limited quantity "rewards" or get in before the doors close on your campaign.

The best nonprofits are able to prompt action throughout the duration of their fundraising campaign. But, the great thing about crowdfunding is that the basic model *encourages* urgency due to the temporal nature of the fundraiser.

It's your job, as a campaign manager, to communicate this emotion to your backers, so that they feel this urgency. Don't just assume they'll feel it. Communicate it. Repeatedly.

The more you create a sense of urgency in the minds of your donors and campaign visitors, the better the chance that they'll actually take action and give money to your case. Of course, this is assuming that you put together a great campaign page. Even with a great page, you'll still raise money, but when you effectively communicate urgency, you'll raise even more money.

Rule #3: Build Relationships at Scale

Okay, I get A LOT of emails and many of them start like this...

"Hey Sal. Love the blog and podcast. Tell me, how do I get strangers to back my campaign?"

First of all, I don't do consulting at the moment and always direct people to my FREE online content. I only provide advice if it benefits the community, like on my forums or the comments section. I wish I could provide it one-on-one, but I simply don't have enough hours in the day.

Second of all, you can't get strangers to back your campaign. However, you can turn strangers into FRIENDS and then get them to back your campaign. It's a subtle distinction.

The way you do this is by building relationships at scale.

Here's the idea summed up. Since everyone thinks *you* want something from them, break the pattern by giving them something *they* want. It has to be something they actually want and it has to add value to their life in some way.

As you begin to provide quality content, advice, or free value, the people will begin to feel like they know you. When someone watches a free video that you put together, they'll get a sense of your values, and eventually, they'll develop an emotional connection with you.

This is EXACTLY why we feel like we "know" big-name YouTubers or celebrities and are completely okay shouting out their name in public or buying something they endorse. In fact, I'd go so far as saying that we feel like we "love" certain comedians because we relate with them so much and almost consider them to be a friend.

We're willing to watch a 5 minute video created by a random person in the world if it makes us say "wow," laugh until we cry, or if it resonates with us and inspires us to be a better person.

When you put out content in the form of videos, emails, social media posts, blog posts, or images that educate, inspire, or entertain, you're investing in the relationship with your potential backers and customers.

Ultimately, you're doing all of this to simply build relationships with multiple people at once. A thousand people can watch one video on your Facebook page and come away feeling like they know a bit more about you and your organization. This is powerful. In the past, you'd have to directly interact one-on-one with the same number of people to create that type of response.

When you do this over a span of time, you can get 1,000 people to subscribe to your email list, or to follow you on a particular social media channel. I know it works, because I've used it to build my own email list to over 20,000 subscribers. I've used these techniques to grow an online forum to over 6,000 users, get over 100 positive iTunes reviews for my podcast, and make a living doing what I love. By the way,

I'm a millennial. When I started, I didn't have what older people label as "experience." If a kid can figure this out, so can you. I'm also giving away the formula. You just have to copy it. Remember, all of this is what gives you the leverage that you need to CRUSH IT during the first week of your nonprofit's fundraising campaign.

Rule #4: Stories Trump Logic

When is the last time that you sat through a two hour long YouTube video lecture? Probably never (though if you have, that's awesome!).

But, people around the world are 100% okay with sitting through a 2 hour movie in a dark room. Even if the movie sucks, they'll stick around because they want to find out what happens.

The same goes for TV shows. How many times have we heard friends say "okay, let's just see what happens and then we'll change the channel." We'll default to this even if it's a trashy show or it isn't good, and we pretty much know what's going to happen.

Stories are powerful for three reasons:

- They create anticipation

- They hold attention

- They encourage empathy with the characters and challenges

If you want someone to feel *exactly* how you felt in a given situation, weave a story around that event. Don't just tell them how you felt.

Quite simply, the best stories *communicate information* and make you *like* or at least feel close to the main character. They are a powerful vehicle for creating trust online.

Not only are they a great way to get people excited about taking action and joining your campaign's community, but they are also super good for seducing journalists and bloggers like me to write about you!

Many of the successful crowdfunding campaigners that I've had on my podcast pitched me with a compelling story, which I then wanted to share with the podcast listeners.

I hate to break it to you, but no one is going to remember the statistics you put out, not even your key donors. Statistics are an important way to establish credibility, but they aren't great for arousing strong emotions. But, I can almost guarantee you that EVERYONE will remember a compelling story. The more emotions that someone feels, the more likely they are to remember an event and also take action in the moment.

You should be sharing your story though several mediums and across multiple platforms. I'm not just talking about the social media platforms out there. I'm also referring to your email list, and when you're speaking at events.

A great story will bring listeners into your world, and when they feel what you feel, they're more likely to take the action that you think "makes complete sense." For most nonprofits out there, that's to fight for a particular cause or to right some injustice in the world.

Rule #5: Create the Emotion of "Liking"

Okay, I know that I sound like I'm a robot right now. I really do enjoy analyzing emotions with the rational side of my brain. I also must *strongly emphasize* that the techniques I'm sharing should only be used if you genuinely believe that you have an amazing product that will make other people's lives better.

In Robert Cialdini's seminal book, Influence, he reveals 3 key points, that I'll highlight below:

- "We like people who are similar to us in terms of opinions, personality traits, background, or lifestyle."

- "Familiarity also plays a role in decisions. Seeing or experiencing something more and becoming familiar with it leads to greater liking."

- "A halo effect occurs when one positive characteristic of a person dominates the way that person is viewed by others. We assign favorable traits to good looking people without logic."

In case you missed kindergarten, when we like someone we are more likely to help them, support them, and take the time to listen to what they have to say.

I'm not saying that you should try to force people to like you or to not be genuine. I'm saying that you should be aware of the emotions that your words, imagery, video, and content creates.

Making a joke in your video might make *you* nervous, but it might make *them* laugh, feel good about themselves, and like you more.

If you're speaking to a group of programmers, you're probably going to generate a great feeling of "liking" if you yourself are also a programmer, can make inside jokes, or relate to the job lifestyle. If you're a business guy who doesn't know the first thing about programming and you assume certain things or butcher key terms, it's unlikely that the audience will see you in a favorable light.

Being focused on how much your donors like you or your team is another great way to avoid typical objections that bog down many nonprofits.

For example, a skeptical donor might harp on the negative qualities of online giving with regards to credit card security. Let's be honest though, online security is a reality. This is innovation we're talking about. You then have to deal with that objection.

If that donor likes you, then they are going to approach the campaign from an entirely different mindset. Maybe instead of focusing on *that* particular aspect, they'll smile at what you're trying to accomplish, decide to support it, and rationalize that you're a good guy so you will be forthright with issues that you or they encounter.

Of course, you should be 100% transparent and forthright with any complications. Just keep in mind that the degree to which someone likes you will affect how they rationalize the things that you ask of them.

To sum it all up, you don't want to come off as some faceless organization with a big board of directors that is just looking to raise money. Personalize it. You want to come off as an actual human being, and in the best-case scenario, as a likeable friend.

These key rules form the bedrock of a sound marketing strategy, which I'll be covering next. You should always have them at the back of your mind when you're engaged in donor communications. They're used every day by marketers to sell products to the public. They aren't just for businesses though. You can steal them and apply these techniques to getting visitors to take action and donate to your online fundraising campaign. They're proven to influence the only thing that matters, getting your donors to *take action.*

Chapter 4:

Fundraising Strategies and Hacks

In the last few chapters, we've explored the psychology behind charitable giving. You now know the emotions that you gotta trigger if you want to encourage someone to give money to your nonprofit organization. But, what do you actually do?

How do you structure your ask?

How do you stop feeling hella' awkward every time you ask for a donation?

How do you get people to connect with your cause?

I know the feeling. As much as you wanna help a cause, no one likes to solicit donations from their friends, family, or strangers. The right strategy can fundamentally change your fundraising efforts. I hate to say it, but it can mean the difference between growing and fading out of existence. With this chapter, I'm going to clear away all those negative feelings and make fundraising simple, easy, and even a little fun!

Your Story Is the ONLY Thing That Matters

When I first heard about "crafting a story" I thought it was complete B.S. Who cares about your story? Why would anyone actually want to know about you or your org's values?

Story is a marketer's dream. You can think of your story as a Trojan Horse. It's an innocent way to allow potential donors to EMOTIONALLY connect with your organization and your cause. There are sooo many nonprofit organizations, and even more people trying to be heard online. The only way to stand out is to cause an emotional reaction in the reader, viewer, or potential donor.

Overall, it doesn't matter how many people that you reach online. What matters is whether or not you reach the right people. It's all about engagement.

When someone hears a story, they deeper their empathy with the main characters. They gain a new perspective on life and the meaning behind it. They come away feeling like they know more about you and your values.

A great book that I read recently on this topic is called "Winning the Story Wars: Why Those Who Tell – and Live – the Best Stories Will Rule the Future," by Jonah Sachs. I highly recommend it if you want to learn how to use stories to influence your donors. A compelling story is the bedrock of a successful marketing and fundraising campaign.

In the book, Sachs gives one great example to help illustrate this point. He shares how most nonprofits will hold up statistics and dry numbers to try to persuade members of the public to care about the cause.

Wrong strategy!

This is also a common mistake that many nonprofits make. Instead, Sachs offers a different approach, which appeals to the emotional side of the brain, rather than the logical side. You can listen to our podcast interview here.

Story is powerful, man. It can get people invested in you and your business. It can make onlookers feel exactly as you felt when creating your unique product, service, or solution.

Rather than looking at story as something that's reserved to the world of fiction authors and Hollywood movies, I want to introduce story as a vehicle for making people care about your crowdfunding campaign. By following this 3-step framework, you'll craft a powerful product story. You can use this technique for a nonprofit campaign. You can also use it for other initiatives.

First, you're going to want to talk about the emotions that surround the particular issue you're trying to solve in society. In this portion of the story, you're painting a picture of how it is for an incredibly disadvantaged group of people. You're using video, images, and storytelling to create emotional empathy with the viewer.

This story may also have characters or individuals that your nonprofit is aimed at helping. A "character" doesn't have to have a rigid definition. All that it refers to is the people in your story. That might be you, your target demographic, or people who are appearing in your video.

The minute you start telling a story, viewers begin to empathize with the various characters. They might like some and not others. We all have experienced rooting for the main character in his quest against the villain. In donate to your nonprofit, someone must know, like, and trust you. The way that you accomplish this transformation in the shortest amount of time is through storytelling.

As you win a viewer over, they begin to lower their mental defensive barriers and at least consider the solution that you've created which will solve a critical problem in society, whether that's global warming, human trafficking, animal cruelty, or gender inequality.

The next step is to tell the story of how and why you have decided to combat this problem in society. What is the solution that you've come up with? Why are you so gosh darn passionate about it? Paint a picture of the struggles and challenges your team had to overcome in order to provide badly needed services to your target demographic.

During this phase of the storytelling process, you're showcasing your values, passion, beliefs, and ability to execute on your vision. The more you tell the story, the more viewers will become to relate with you and your team. If you don't believe me, just think back to the last time you were in a movie theater or watching a film from the comfort of your home.

If it was a horror film, you probably felt fear. If it was an action-packed thriller, you may have noticed your heart rate increasing. Sometimes, when there is a surprising event, we'll literally jump or move our body in response.

With certain film techniques, we'll have an emotional reaction simply because the scene is surprising, gory, or scary-looking. However, for most scenes, there needs to be the context of back-story for us to really care about what's going on.

Storytelling makes onlookers feel emotions and put themselves in the shoes of the person experiencing the events.

The third and final part of my 3-step storytelling framework is to show the transformation that you've been able to kindle in the lives, hearts, and souls of the individuals you're helping. In other words, what results are you getting with your nonprofit?

This third step is crucial because it proves to onlookers that you can actually do what you say you're gonna do. You're going to be wise with their donations. You're going to put it to good use and actually impact the world. There are so many nonprofits out there that want to help, but many of them are inefficient and ineffective.

When you talk about the positive results that you've been able to have in society, it makes someone feel completely comfortable about donating to your cause. They now know that you're the real deal. They don't feel skeptical. They feel excited. They can't wait to help other people on this planet. They've been searching out ways to and they've finally come across and authentic organization that's making an impact. What's more, it's an impact they care about.

Your Vision is The Opposite of Your Story

Your story is all about where you've been and how it's made you into who you are today.

Your vision is where you're going. It's the type of world that you want to live in.

Everyone connects with a good story. A great story will maintain our attention for hours on end and generate discussion amongst our friends. We connect with characters and stories that hold up values that we agree with.

But, a story is not enough to motivate grand-scale action. That's where your vision comes in.

A great vision will motivate thousands of volunteers to toil day and night towards a goal. Effective CEOs and leaders know this well.

What is YOUR vision? How can you communicate it in a tangible way to your donors?

When we all agree on a vision for the world and are emotionally moved by what it could mean for our family and our life, anything is possible.

Believe it or not but crafting a compelling vision for the future is actually a fundraising strategy. That's because it is a form of a "promise." You're promising that when donors give money to your nonprofit that they will causing some kind of change in the world. You're outlining what that donation will do for the future. It's a remarkably effective way of taking donors out of their minute day-to-day life and begin to imagine what the grand scale could be like.

By continually telling your story, you will capture attention and capture rapport with potential donors. By reiterating your vision, you will unite volunteers, donors, and supporters behind your core mission. You'll get them to contribute time and resources in larger ways.

To get started painting your vision, I want you to grab a scrap of paper and list out all of the major changes you'd like to make in the world with your nonprofit. Be as specific and tangible as possible. Get down into the nitty gritty. Then, I want you to write next to each of these items what that would mean for people around the world.

How would that change their everyday life? What would they feel like? Get concrete and really describe it so that anyone could close their eyes and imagine this great future. Once you have a vision that's coming together, begin to practice sharing it. Remember to speak with enthusiasm. Let your excitement for the future be heard in your voice and be shown on your face. It will instantly translate and slowly begin to get them excited and inspired.

Stand Out By Getting CERTIFIED By the Media

The next way to build trust and authority with donors is to get certified or validated by third parties. These could include:

- Partnerships with well-known organizations

- High profile donors

- Get written about in a media publication

Getting in the media is one of my my specialities. I've been cited by the media at a very young age, including The Wall Street Journal, The New York Times, CNN, and more.

In fact, as I was writing this very chapter, I discovered that I was mentioned by Forbes for my work in personal crowdfunding. The article explains how students can use fundraising websites like GoFundMe to raise money for college. I don't share this to brag. I actually think it's silly. Why should people listen to me MORE because I've been written about in some public.

Not only did these and other media hits drive me traffic, but they also elevated my brand. It put me head and shoulders above other casual bloggers. When telling a story online, the most powerful tools are video, images, and social proof. As we discussed in the last chapter, social proof simply refers to the tendency for donors to pay attention to something when other people are paying attention to it.

For example, if a bunch of your friends are giving to one particular organization, or are liking a video on Facebook, you're more likely to take the time to check out that organization.

By incorporating testimonials and by encouraging tangible signs of activity around your fundraiser, you will command greater attention in the eyes of potential donors. By making testimonials like more prominent, it will be easier to convince skeptical donors of the value of giving money to your nonprofit.

If one of your donors is really happy for having participated in one of your fundraisers or events, put them on camera. Capture that emotion. The positive emotions they experienced after giving to your nonprofit are the same emotions that your potential donors hope to experience.

Effective Techniques to Ask For Donations

So you've incorporated a story into an "ask." You're starting to work on your vision. You're even starting to collect some forms of social proof, like testimonials, partnership logos, or media mentions. It still doesn't get you away from that ask. You gotta step up and actually ask someone for a donation to your nonprofit. Let's discuss a few ways to make this process easier.

#1: Examine your beliefs about giving

It's tall order, but here me out here. I want to first examine what you think of when you hear the word "solicit."

By its very definition solicit means to:

- ask for or try to obtain something from someone.

- request, seek, apply for

- press for, beg, or plead for

All of these definitions come with negative connotations. No wants to "beg" or "plead" someone. It's humiliating. It's embarrassing.

The idea of trying to "obtain something" from someone or "press someone" for something sounds really manipulative. You're really just after their money, and it makes you feel kinda squeamish.

Before doing any kind of donor outreach, I want you to think about the REAL people you're helping. Think about what the money you raise will mean to them. How will it change their lives?

Not only is it your job to fight for this group to be heard, but it's also your duty.

Now, take a second to think about the nice people who want to help other people. They're out there, right now. They want to help, they just don't know how.

You're giving them the chance of a lifetime! They're able to directly make an impact in the world with their funds. How freakin' cool is that?

To successfully persuade someone to give money to your nonprofit, you must genuinely:

1. Believe it is a good choice for them that will enhance their life

2. Be committed to helping the target demographic or your cause

3. Be willing to put your own ego aside in order to fulfill your duty

It's the kind of motivation that a parent gets when they see their child was treated unfairly. At that moment in time, the parent's ego doesn't matter. It's only about taking action to right a wrong in their child's life.

#2: Tie money to benefits

I guarantee you, no one wants to give money to charity.

Wait… what!?

Yep. No one cares about giving money to charity.

People care about HELPING other people. The charity is just the intermediary.

The best thing that you can do to get a donation from a stranger is to tie that donation to a tangible result that you're causing in someone else's life.

For example:

- $25 will give 200 gallons of water to children in Africa

- $100 will save 10 stray dogs from being euthanized

- $500 will give a starving family food for an entire year

You can also have a sliding scale. If people want to have a bigger impact, they can increase their donation.

By doing this, you're making the impact more real in their mind. You can picture 10 stray dogs or the idea of a family going without hunger for a year. It's harder to picture giving $500 to a charity out of the kindness of your heart.

The more you can create an image in someone's head as to the real change their making with their money, the more excited they'll be to participate.

#3: People give money to people, not orgs

This is a hard pill to swallow. I love nonprofits as much as the rest of us!

But, to most people, they are strange, unfamiliar, and inefficient. People are skeptical. They don't want to help pay your staff. They want to help people that are actually in need.

We are all very visual creatures. If you can SEE the person you're helping at the moment you decide to give money, it's going to make the whole process at lot smoother.

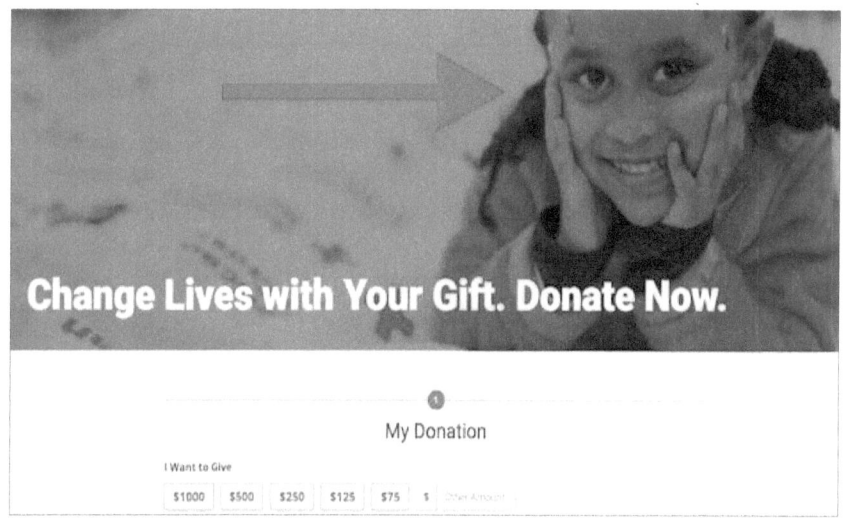

We're basically highly evolved monkeys.

We have multiple parts to our brain. One is the limbic system. This is the emotion-centric part of the brain. It registers a face and we feel emotions.

Then, we have the neocortex, which is responsible for decision making, logic, and self-control. That is the part of the brain that can logically determine a face we see on a computer screen is NOT a real face.

Whether you admit it or not, having a *face* in front of you when you make a donation, it feels *different* than if you're just seeing text and have a sophisticated cognitive perception that you're giving money to a real person.

#4: Keep it Simple Stupid – Ask Directly

Everyone, myself included, is lazy.

We don't want to do WORK. We don't want to have to think. We don't want to have to make decisions in life.

Having to "figure something out" like where a donation button is, how much you should give, or what it goes towards is WORK.

You gotta make it super easy for someone give a donation to your charity. Suggest an amount. Give them the link. Have all the essential info there they need to make a decision.

I would even air on the side of over communicating. At the very worst, someone just won't end up reading a section. At the best, someone who's confused will have something explained to them.

One of the big mistakes that nonprofits make when asking for donations is that they don't really ask. They just kind of hint at it.

They beat around the bush. They tell people about this new fundraiser they're doing. They don't really explain much. They just hope that people take action.

If you want people to consider your proposal, then you have to ask them directly. It doesn't have to be specifically about the amount of money you want, but it does have to be in the form of a question.

Examples include:

- What do you think? Will you help?

- Will you join us?

- Do you care about this cause? Will you give $25 to help?

Before making this ask, the person should be aware of who you are, what the organization does, and the benefits of giving money.

If they are, then great! You've done your job. You can't force someone to give money, you can only see what objections they have and address them.

Some people will say "yeah, sure, I'll give!" Others will say things like:

- Not sure. Is this website secure?

- Can I give cash?

- Maybe next month

These are objections. They can be overcome with the right strategic approach, but that's beyond the scope of this chapter.

#5: Ask when emotion is high

Have you ever been in a frame of mind where you're not at all willing to entertain suggestions, ideas, or other points of view? Maybe you're mad, drained, or just not emotionally available?

Other people feel the SAME WAY. They're not always in the right frame of mind to donate money.

The reverse is also true. Sometimes, people are in an extremely receptive frame of mind. They're feeling positive, joyous, and generous. They want to help.

You can see how the world's collective "state of mind" also cycles as we near certain holidays, like Christmas. People feel in more of a giving mood. They might remember the teachings of their religion and are feeling more generous. When you're on the phone, in person, at events, or chatting with someone, try to put them in the right state of mind before making the big ask. Your ask will have a higher chance of success.

#6: Segment your donor database

Each donor is a unique human being with interests, preferences, and desires. Many nonprofits are making the mistake of sending the same communications to each of them. Instead, you're going to want to tailor your communications based on the segmentation of your donor database.

According to Women's Philanthropy Institute, 70% of giving circles are comprised of women. The organization went on to say that for women, giving is more about an empathetic connection to the end individual, whereas with men, it's more about self-interest. Neither reason for giving is better than the other, but an email or landing page would look different for each group.

In addition, when looking through the Global Trends in Giving Report, you'll see a clear breakdown of the actual causes that genders care most about. Women care most about:

- Children and youth (15%)

- Animals and wildlife (13%)

- Health and wellness (10%)

- Human and social services (8%)

- Hunger and homelessness (8%)

Knowing this, it would be smarter to target women online when your fundraiser is related to animals and wildlife. Your messaging, call-to-actions, and overall design of your website could be tailored to this demographic. There is also a clear breakdown for the causes that men care most about:

- Children and youth (15%)

- Health and wellness (11%)

- Human and social services (9%)

- Faith and spirituality (8%)

- Hunger and homelessness (8%)

Of course, there are some similarities in male and female giving patters, but there are also some differences. If you want to get the best ROI (return on investment) out of your marketing and fundraising efforts, then it makes sense to tailor your messaging for the main demographic that you're going after.

Segmentation of an email list or a CRM (customer relationship management) database is *standard practice* in the for-profit world. When you're launching a new product, you're hyper-aware of the demographic that's most likely to turn into buyers. The same type of effective marketing practices can be applied to online fundraising. It will decrease a cash-strapped nonprofit's marketing costs and allow them to double down on what's working.

In this chapter, we covered a few effective ways to get strangers to donate to your nonprofit organization. We broke down some simple techniques for getting them to believe in your mission, trust your ability to pull it off, and actually give you a donation. Next, we're going to get into a few simple ways that you can actually increase the traffic to your nonprofit website. This makes it easier to increase your overall revenue to support your operations.

Chapter 5:

Marketing Your Fundraiser

Online marketing is one of the most confusing subjects out there. Not only are there a slew of different social media platforms, but the demand for a donor's attention is stretched thinner than ever before. You have to compete with funny cat videos on Facebook, entertaining YouTubers, Instagram fitness models, and more for the only thing that matters, a prospective donor's *attention*.

Thankfully, I've figured out the best ways to market an online fundraiser and I'm going to share them with you in this chapter. These are tried and true techniques that are proven to work! Keep in mind that every nonprofit is different. You might find that you're seeing more results through one marketing channel than another. Don't worry! This is a *good* thing. Half of the battle is figuring out where your audience is and how to reach them. The other half is figuring out what they care about.

There are three main ways to get attention online. I like to segment one's online audience into a few different categories. Ultimately, these buckets come down to how people spend their time on their laptop and on their smartphone. A good marketing strategy will incorporate all of these elements, but the first is the most important.

Rule #1: Your Email List is King.

Your email list is the Holy Grail of all of your marketing activity. Why? According to Mckinsey & Company, "Email conversion rates are three times higher than social media, with a 17% higher value in the conversion."

The individuals who sign up for your email list are not simply numbers, part of a statistic on your email provider's dashboard, or passive donors. They are real human beings with thoughts, feelings, desires, and emotions.

Email is still the #1 marketing channel out there for getting donors to take action. It's completely replaced the old-school way of sending out marketing messages to physical mailing addresses. Think of email as the "home-base" where most donors receive information about the topics that they care about.

Tomorrow, Facebook could change their algorithm so that no one sees your posts. Your website could be hacked. You could find that your Instagram profile is banned for some reason. But, you'll always have your email list.

If you have 1,000 people subscribed to your email list, then 1,000 individuals have raised their hand saying, "I want to receive messages from your nonprofit organization." Think of a room with 1,000 people in it. That would be a massive crowd!

The reason that email is so powerful is because it allows you to direct traffic to a *designated place* at a *specific* time. You don't have to wait for people to see your messages on social media, which might be drowned out by all their other social media messages. Instead, they can all check out your crowdfunding campaign at the same time and make a donation. This is why many campaigns see so much activity and so many donations during the first day of their launch, which usually spills into the next two days.

In order to get more email subscribers, you need to understand a bit of the psychology behind subscribing to an email list.

Use an email list provider, not a temporary solution.

I know that money is tight, which is why you're planning on launching a crowdfunding campaign in the first place in order to finance your nonprofit organization! However, it would be a huge mistake to not use an established email list management provider, like MailChimp, which is free up until 2,000 subscribers, or Aweber, which has been around for a while and has great functionality.

Why? Email list software will:

- Give you analytics every time you send a campaign regarding the number of people who click links, open that email, unsubscribe, and more.

- Let you create auto-responders every time someone opts into your email list to direct them to a page or convey a message (like the one I've set up with my newsletter).

- Make it super easy to set up a series of pre-scheduled messages, which can be a great way to automate some of the marketing process as you lead up to the launch of your campaign.

- See who most frequently opens your emails.

Offer value in exchange for an email address

What is "value?" You're right. That's a very abstract concept.

Basically, by giving your potential subscriber something exclusive or beneficial, he or she will be more likely to subscribe to your email list because they will get something out of the relationship.

For example, you could use MailChimp to direct the subscriber to:

- A behind-the-scenes special video.

- Deliver an exclusive invite to a fundraising gala.

- Send them a link to a poll or special FB group where they can vote on something related to your organization.

- Get an exclusive discount code that will give them 10% off of the products or services of partner companies.

- View an awesome hilarious company video "beware: don't watch this video for our upcoming fundraising campaign while you are at work, or you will burst out laughing."

Think of these value-adding ideas as mini rewards that are meant to gain the interest of a potential subscriber so that they are more comfortable exchanging their email address for future announcements regarding the launch of your nonprofit's fundraising campaign.

Make your email-opt in noticeable.

Ask yourself three questions:

- Where is the email opt-in form on your website?

- What is the first thing that should draw a visitor's attention when they visit your site?

- Why did a visitor come to your website in the first place?

Now, ask these questions to a series of visitors that you've connected with (friends, family, individuals who are interested in your project).

You might know where your email opt-in form is, but do they? You might want to direct their attention to a particular video, link, or email opt-in form the moment that they visit your website, but what actually is grabbing their attention?

Determining how your visitor discovered your website in the first place, whether it was through social media, a search engine, an article you've written, or an event you attended, will help you figure out the type of content that you should offer them in exchange for subscribing to your newsletter.

For example, if someone discovered your website from an inspirational video that you posted on social media, which will be a part of a larger online awareness mission, then it's likely that they'd love to receive more content like this!

Resources to help track this information:

- Google analytics.

- Bitly links.

- CrazyEgg heat map and click tracking.

- Mouseflow mouse tracking.

Use call to actions (ask people to subscribe).

This might seem silly, but you'd be surprised the amount of email subscribers that websites lose out on simply because they forget to ask a visitor to subscribe!

One way to put this in perspective is to watch YouTubers who have millions of subscribers and who have made a living out of making online videos. What's the last thing that they say at the end of every video? It's something along the lines of "if you enjoyed this video, take a moment to give it a thumbs up or leave a comment." They might also say "subscribe if you'd like more funny prank videos like this!"

ABSYL: Always be selling your list, meaning, always be highlighting why people should subscribe, particularly if they've taken the time to watch one of your videos, read through a blog post, or go visit your website.

Don't just tell people what you want, which is to subscribe to your email list. Explain to them why it's awesome for them if they subscribe.

Build a landing page

A landing page is very different from a full-blown website, which has all of the information about your team, your mission, and your journey. The purpose of a landing page is to solely to collect an email address or have your visitor take an action, rather than exposing them to lots of information about your company or project.

You might set the landing page as your homepage leading up to the launch of your nonprofit's crowdfunding campaign or even have a custom domain name that you reference on business cards or should you attend any conventions, do interviews, or get linked to by a media publication.

A great landing page will share compelling information about your upcoming project in an organized fashion and highlight any multimedia that you have (video, images), the benefits of being a participant in your upcoming your launch or what's meaningful about the mission, and more.

Tools to help you build a landing page:

- LaunchRock

- Unbounce

- LeadPages

- OptimizePress (if using WordPress – more complex).

- Free: Use WordPress and a landing page theme.

Consider WordPress-Based Plugins

If you're not using WordPress as the framework for your website, then this step won't be helpful. However, if you are, then I highly recommend checking out the OptinMonster and OptinSkin plugins, which I use on this website and others.

If you're using MailChimp as your mailing list provider, you could also enable "evil popup mode," but I don't find this to be as affective in terms of providing data or cool themes as the above two plugins.

These plugins will draw more attention to your message which prompt visitors to subscribe to your email list.

Drive traffic and measure results

I've highlighted a few tools and techniques to get more email list subscribers in anticipation of your crowdfunding campaign launch. Ultimately, the only way to get more subscribers is to drive traffic to your website or landing page and adjust the positioning/wording of the call-to-action messaging that you're using to get a visitor to subscribe to your email list.

This could mean that you might need to use trial and error to figure out the type of incentive that gets a visitor most excited about signing up for your email list, or the content that you're putting out to get people on to your website in the first place.

Rule #2: Have a social media presence everywhere, get followers, and automate.

The nonprofit industry is historically slow to adopt new technologies. Instead, organizations stay with tried and true methods, like mailing out brochures to potential donors in a community. Investing some time to learn how to build up followers on your social media accounts will be well worth it in the future when you have a bunch of interested individuals with whom you can share your new campaign!

I'd define the main social media networks as:

- **Facebook.** Facebook is one of the largest social media networks out there with 1.71 billion monthly active users in 2016. Key trends are mobile adoption, video consumption on Facebook, and the changing Facebook algorithm.

- **LinkedIn.** LinkedIn is the largest professional social network with 450 million members. The platform has growth a lot in the last few years, with the introduction of articles and content on the website.

- **Instagram.** While I don't think Instagram is as mature as Facebook with paid marketing tools, it's still a very powerful network to gain followers and get people interested in your cause.

- **Twitter.** Finally, many have argued that Twitter is a waning social network, but I don't agree. There are still a large number of people who get their news from Twitter and check it daily.

You could also look into networks like Snapchat and Pinterest, but I wouldn't include these in the main list. Ultimately, you'll probably narrow in on one or two of these social networks in the long-run. My Twitter is certainly much stronger than my Instagram. You'll find the network that is the best fit for your organization, but you should have a presence on all of them!

Now that we've outlined most of the major networks, you're probably wondering…how are you actually going to get followers? How are you going to get people to take time out of their day to follow you and receive messages related to your nonprofit organization?

You won't be using social media to share thoughts like "My cat just rolled over." You will be using social media as a tool to figure out what type of content your audience likes and what causes they care about.

As a rudimentary example, let's say you are trying to start a nonprofit to help educate children in El Salvador and you shared a post on Facebook of a child and his mother reading, which also had an inspirational caption. If it got lots of clicks and shares, that tells you that potential donors are moved by images like these.

You may consider creating similar content on your nonprofit's blog and then sharing it. In the long-term, it would attract readers to the blog, who are also part of your donor base. You will then have the opportunity to ask them to donate to your upcoming crowdfunding campaign.

There are two words that sums up why people will follow you: content marketing.

You're going to be putting out content that will either be informative/useful or entertaining. Informative content could take the form of articles, tips, ideas, and advice that you share to help them achieve their goals in some way. Entertaining content could take the form of quotes, images, shocking or inspiring facts, etc. This type of content is emotional. People will follow you based on how they perceive you will make them feel in the future. You may make them feel inspired, motivated, or hungry to reach their goals.

By continually putting out free content that resonates, you'll begin to build an audience on these different social media platforms. Yes, this takes time. Accumulating followers and improving audience engagement doesn't happen overnight. If you're just getting started, plan for this to be an eight month to a year-long process before you begin getting some momentum. In that span of time, you will figure out what types of content works best for your audience, when the best time to post is, which social media channels are a good fit for your nonprofit, and you will gain an in-depth understanding of the problems that your customers care about.

Eventually, you'll start to mix in your own "call to action" messages on social media, like asking people to back your crowdfunding campaign. But, you shouldn't start here. The primary focus should be to get people to follow your social media profile to get notified when more content comes out.

I've used this simple strategy to build up thousands of followers on Instagram, Facebook, and Twitter. However, it does get difficult to keep up with all that work! That's why I've automated most of my social media marketing.

Tools to automate your social media

I'm horrible at being consistent. Even my tennis coach used to say, "Sal, you need to be more consistent! You're great one day and have a bad day the next."

Thankfully, when it comes to social media marketing, there are lots of tools out there that will allow you to pre-schedule social media messages that will go out in the future. This means that you can sit down and spend two hours planning out all the social media messages that will be shared on your

Facebook page for the next month. Then, you don't have to worry about it for the rest of the month.

I'd recommend looking into:

Hootsuite: A powerful social tool to save time managing multiple social networks. If you haven't heard of it, it's a tool that you can use to schedule Tweets and Facebook posts ahead of time on your phone or on your computer.

Buffer: Buffer is a Hootsuite competitor and lets you manage your Twitter, Facebook, and LinkedIn social profiles. Buffer makes it super easy to share any page you're reading. Keep your Buffer topped up and it will automagically share them for you through the day

The great thing about these two tools is that they also come with analytical capabilities. I personally use Buffer, which tells me how many people are clicking on the links in my posts, sharing them, and which posts are seeing the most engagement. I can also re-schedule posts to go out.

Rule #3: Get free traffic from the media

Leveraging the media is a great way to get free traffic to your nonprofit organization, particularly if you're running a crowdfunding campaign. First, I'm going to cover what to include in a press release. Second, I'll talk about direct outreach. Last, I'll cover a few press release tools out there.

When drafting a PR campaign for your fundraising campaign, it's important to keep in mind how online marketing differs from the launch of a traditional in-person fundraising event. Although there are a lot of crowdfunding sites out there, many of them have the following elements in common.

Fundraising Duration: Almost every crowdfunding campaign has a set duration, which will impact the amount of time that you have to take advantage of any PR attention or media hits. Therefore, you need to be super organized when drafting a PR outreach strategy. Some media publications will offer the "embargo" option if they like your project and want to write about it. Basically, this means that they will hold off on the publication of the article until a certain date.

Rewards and Perks: The rewards and perks offered throughout a crowdfunding campaign are a great way to incentivize lurkers to become donors. Some of your donors might care about the mission of your project, like you, or find your video engaging. Others will simply want to learn about what kinds of perks you're offering. Make sure to include these in your press release. Also, underscoring the "limited" or "scarce" nature of them and how to claim one is a great call to action for people to check out your campaign.

Social Proof: Backers are more skeptical than ever! Unfortunately, a growing number of campaigns have defrauded donors or have simply not fulfilled on their promises. Therefore, any way that you can add social proof or credibility to the campaign will make it more likely that journalists will check out the project or that potential backers will. Social proof can include the number of social shares, donors, comments, or dollars given. Credibility can include media mentions, partner organizations, or simply a compelling founder story.

Here are a few items that you should keep in mind when creating the PR draft for the launch of your crowdfunding campaign.

Do you have an eye-catching headline? In the same way that click-bait news headlines give readers a reason to click through the story, you want to have an interesting headline for your press release and the subject of your email so that a journalist has a reason to read further.

Have you included images or multimedia? Words are one way to tell a story. Images and video are other ways to get a story across very quickly in this social media driven and attention starved world. Have high resolution images on hand that the journalist or blogger can use in their article. Often times, the number of images or multimedia you can send is limited, so provide a link where they can find more multimedia assets.

Are there quotes from the founder or team? Have you ever noticed how news or human-interest stories tend to include quotes from sources or the founder themselves if it's a new nonprofit organization? Rather than making the journalist call you up or exchange emails for an interesting quote, include that quote in your press release! You can also include testimonials from donors or partners to add to the social proof of the pitch.

Is it easy to find relevant links and contact information? I can't tell you the number of times that I've been emailed asking to cover a story and the email didn't have a link to the company's website or the URL of where I can find the campaign. Make it as easy as possible for journalists to find where your campaign exists online. They might be on their mobile phone and not want to search around to find it.

Have you answered the who, what, when, where, why and how? It's true that the press release should spin an enthralling story and make the journalist envision how awesome of a story this would make. However, it also needs to include concrete facts, like when the campaign will end (or start), what the product is, who designed it, and why they are so passionate about this project.

How hard to read is the press release? It's always best to put yourself in the shoes of someone reading the press release. Is the information easily digestible? Are the paragraphs short and to the point? Are you using active verbs and strong grammar? One easy way to get an idea of how well it's written is to read it out loud! You'll quickly catch any grammar or spelling errors. You'll also get an idea of how the sentences flow.

What emotions do you arouse in the reader? Finally, a press release is part art and part science. Ask a friend in your industry (or familiar with your industry) to read your press release and ask them how they feel after having read the story behind the fundraising effort. Are they excited to learn more? Bored? Are they confused? Simple questions like these will give you an idea of the tweaks you might need to make to elicit the desired emotional response.

With your press release, you need to identify how your latest crowdfunding campaign fits into the hot topics and trends that journalists and bloggers are writing about.

For example, right now, teaching coding in inner-city schools is gaining traction. There are niche blogs writing about programming, education, and STEM. There are also larger publications creating content about the technology industry.

If you created a nonprofit crowdfunding campaign to help educate kids about coding, you may want to consider contacting publications that have written about these topics, as you are a prime example of a growing trend and therefore newsworthy.

Again, how does your story fit into the overall global discussion? What trends are you a part of? Research the publications engaged in these trends.

The other thing that I'll say before we get into contacting journalists is that you must appeal to multiple audiences.

Does your nonprofit organization use a new teaching technique that will have a big impact on a particular industry? What organizations will benefit down the road if your campaign raises the needed funds?

For example, when Arnold Schwarzenegger was working to attract media attention for his breakout film Conan the Barbarian, he appealed to multiple audiences in order to get the ink needed to fill theaters.

"To promote the movie, it was important to work every possible angle. We used special-interest magazines to build an audience – stories on sword fighting for the martial-arts magazines. Stories for horse magazines. Stories for swords and sorcery. Stories for bodybuilding magazines on how you needed top conditioning to be Conan." – Total Recall: My Unbelievably True Life Story

Let's start to talk about how you can directly contact journalists and get them to write about your crowdfunding campaign. Email is still the preferred method of contact, but

I've also seen campaigners get media stories by contacting journalists via Twitter and LinkedIn.

How do you stand out from the crowd?

According to a survey conducted by BuzzSumo, Journalists receive 25-100 pitches via email per day and countless more on social media. In order to stand out, it's best to avoid cliché buzzwords and stick to a succinct, straight-forward, and relevant pitch.

Be succinct. Get to the point, and if needed, use bullet-points to highlight the major reasons why this news is important and a good fit for the publication. Don't write an essay. Your email should be scannable.

Be straight-forward. Avoid PR buzzwords that only serve to make it more difficult to understand your story and why it's a good fit for the publication. Otherwise, you will sound like all the other nonprofits pitching the journalist and fail to stand out.

Be relevant – Why this journalist, why your company, and why does this story matter now? Don't just copy and paste generic emails. Tailor your pitch to both the reporter and the publication.

When is the best time to pitch a reporter?

After conducting several informal interviews, PrDaily put together an awesome breakdown of the best time(s) to reach out to a journalist. Overwhelmingly, all of the reporters surveyed preferred to be pitched via email in the early morning. However, due to the large volume of weekend mail, the participants also suggested to wait until Tuesday, once the Monday rush was over and they had more time to look over each email.

This information is corroborated by MarketConsensus, who also recommended sending pitch emails between 8 am – 11 am and to avoid Mondays.

Should you send mass emails and if so, when?

Despite the overwhelming industry advice not to send mass emails, I've actually gotten responses from them and have gotten stories as a result of them. Many journalists may not like these practices, but they can work if you have a killer headline, pitch, and are going after a bunch of publications with a similar audience.

However, I do think they should be used in conjunction with direct pitching and relationship building. That being said, if you're going to send out a mass email with services like PRWeb, MyPrGenie, PRNewswire, SBWire, or others, then take into account the best time to send that email. Subscribers' top engagement times are 8 a.m. – 10 a.m. and 3 p.m. – 4 p.m. with up to 6.8% average open rates and CTR (click through rate).

PR goes to experts in their space

Sometimes when you're marketing a new fundraising effort, it's easy to forget that you're in "this" for the long haul, whether that's growing your nonprofit or starting a new one.

In my experience, experts in their space will never have to worry about getting PR. What was the first thing that happened on TV when Malaysia Airlines Flight 370 disappeared? The media brought aviation experts on to comment about the event and the implications.

Experts are cited in the media all the time! Even I was quoted in a recent CNN interview. The important thing is to put yourself out there as an expert, so that you can seize these opportunities for some free PR.

HARO is a great free resource for these types of PR hits.

How can you frame yourself as an expert in your space and use that as an angle for a story, or to get some free PR indirectly?

87% of Reporters love data, facts, and figures.

Have you ever noticed when a "new study" is released that analyzes data points to corroborate or highlight an interesting trend, it goes viral on news outlets?

How can you enhance your pitch with facts, figures, and data? How does your nonprofit fit into a larger cultural trend?

Backing up your vision and story with numbers is a great way to snag attention away from other pitchers, just pushing their "game changing" initiative.

P.S. Just kidding about the 87%

Journalists must write about things they don't want to.

I'll tell you a little secret. Journalists don't necessarily want to write about every story, but sometimes they have to.

You're really going to tell me that if a holiday is coming around, like Christmas, that a publication isn't going to look for Christmas stories? Or if a particular story is blowing up like the The Ice Bucket Challenge, an editor isn't going to say, "I want this story on my desk by ____."

Newspapers are in the business of attracting eyeballs and advertisement dollars. Most major publications always need to write about what is trending or be left out of the flow of online and mobile traffic.

The question is: How can you fit yourself into the stories that are trending or a holiday that is coming up? You need to begin to think about what kinds of stories reporters will be looking for given the time of the year and what's happening in the current media discussion.

Repeat business = success.

There is a big difference between a nonprofit organization that has repeat donors and one-time donors. The same is true for PR. Rather than seeking one-time transactional relationships, it's best to develop a long-term relationship with a journalist, who may move publications in the future or be able to forward you along to his or her friends (who are also journalists).

You should take a long-term view of PR outreach. Why? This is exactly what a PR agency does, and they are in the business of getting their clients stories. Why wouldn't you take the same approach as a professional PR firm?

A relationship with even a handful of reporters can yield dividends down the road. Going out of your way to be helpful and connecting them with sources or people in your industry they'd like to speak to can be a good way to start.

Your headline must be clickable

It's hard to have a clickable headline without knowing your audience, which brings us back to point #1 (relevancy).

Ideally, your headline should be tailored to the individual reporter or publication.

Your name and headline are the first few things a reporter is going to see when they look at your email. How can you phrase the headline to get them interested in learning more?

One technique I've found to be helpful is to see if there are any headline commonalities in other articles that have been published by that reporter and then craft your email subject to be similar to those headlines.

There is no blueprint.

Although there are "best practices" and mistakes to avoid, getting PR is a learning process. You need to figure out what works well for your company and your industry, which will take time.

Personally, I've had experiences that fly in the face of the common industry advice in terms of the ideal times to send emails and how to best do journalist outreach. Keep in mind that these are general guidelines and are not set in stone.

I think the most worthwhile takeaway you should get from this section is that you need to adopt a PR mindset.

You need to begin to observe the news, TV, and print media and begin to form questions. Why did a publication quote this expert, or why did this reporter choose to write about this particular story? Beginning to make yourself aware of the inner workings of the news media will help you begin to become active on the pitching side.

Press release websites:

- CrowdfundingPr.org (free)

- PRLog (free)

- Free Press Release (free)

- 188PressRelease (free)

- 24-7 Press Release (free)

- Pr.com (free)

- i-NewsWire (paid)

- PrWeb (paid)

- PrNewswire (paid)

- BusinessWire (paid)

In this chapter, you discovered a few surefire ways to market your nonprofit and a crowdfunding campaign. We also went through a few key tools that you can use to make the process much easier. These techniques will only work if you take action and actually implement them! You have to start now. Start building your email list, social media profiles, and start developing a relationship with journalists. You'll thank me later!

Chapter 6:

The Holy Grail of Fundraising

This is what you've been waiting for!

Every nonprofit is on a quest. A journey in search of the Holy Grail. It's that unlimited, self-replenishing treasure chest that *never* goes empty. You've heard stories about this mythological artifact, but you're unsure if it actually exists. You've been brought to near exhaustion on your voyage, scavaging the earth for it. But, you've yet to find it. Little did you know, it's always been at your fingertips.

Imagine what it would be like if you never had to worry about fundraising *ever again.*

How would that change your life? How would that change your career?

Most importantly, how could that enable you to affect the lives of those you help? Chances are, it would be pretty profound!

If you are able to master what I'm about to share in this chapter, then you will tap into that infinite resource of fundraising cash that's available to *any* nonprofit. This is the doorway to a better and more efficient way of fundraising that will blow the lid off your skeptics. It's the tool that you can use to truly impact the world. You just have to be willing to open that door.

The Fundraising Funnel

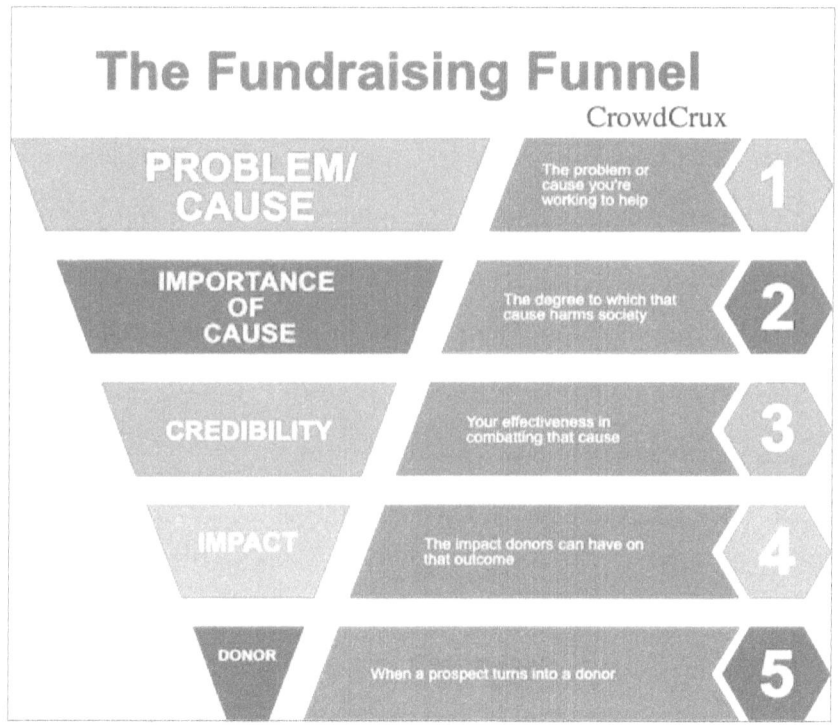

Let's start off with the biggest problem – turning a stone-cold stranger into a raving fan, supporter, volunteer, and nonprofit donor. Did you know that 31% of donors worldwide that give to nonprofits and charities do so to orgs located outside of their country of residence (Global Trends in Giving Report). Why would someone give someone to a nonprofit that's on the other side of the world? It's because they first connect with the problem or cause that you're trying to remedy.

There are so many problems that exist in the world. Devastation of the rainforest. Starving children in third-world countries. The need for adequate social services. The importance of health and wellness in impoverished communities. If your nonprofit or cause is not centered around a real problem, then it will be virtually impossible to raise money. As we've already covered, donors give money to alleviate *pain* that others feel. Those donors empathize with those individuals and wanna help.

This is the very point where you capture the *attention* of a prospective donor. They start to pay attention to the problem that you're working to remedy. After you have their attention, in their head, they begin to assess the importance of that cause. In other words, do your messages deserve their continued attention. When it comes to importance, this can be boiled down to two things: the stakes and the relevancy.

By stakes, I mean, what will happen if this problem continues to go unchecked. How will it affect people around the world, children, families, and affect future generations? Is it a minor problem or a major one? By relevancy I mean the degree to which the effects of this problem are related to the individual's life. A person living in Massachusetts might not be willing to give to a homeless shelter in Utah, but they might be willing to give to one in Lowell, their local hometown. That donor cares about the issue of homelessness and starvation, but they're more willing to give money to a nonprofit helping a local community that's more relevant to them.

Relevancy can go beyond just physical location. It can also take the form of the social group that you belong to. It can include the experiences you've gone through in life that make up your identity. These life experiences are what allow us to relate to other people who have different cultural values. For example, if you were in the armed forces, you're going to be more likely to give to a charity that is helping soldiers who suffer from PTSD. If you're a mother who's been through a traumatic experience, then you're going to be willing to help other mothers who have been through a similar one (or to help prevent them from going through it).

However, it's not enough to just have a cause with high stakes and relevancy. Your organization and you, the messenger, must also be *credible.* While the former two variables will get someone to pay attention to you and get them to want to help, credibility will check that logical box in their mind that says, "okay this charity is legit." All human beings have feelings. Emotionally, we want things. But, we're smart enough to know that we need to think through our thoughts before taking action. Our critical faculties prevent us from making stupid decisions. Basically, we do some mental arithmetic to make sure we aren't getting carried away by our own imaginations.

When you are credible in the eyes of a donor (which we covered in Mastering Donor Psychology), then the opportunity you present will bypass the critical faculty of your potential donor. They will be willing to keep reading, keep watching, or go to the next step to see how they can participate in the activities of your nonprofit organization.

This will lead into the next phase of their logical analysis: evaluating their potential impact.

Human beings like to visibly *see* the impact that their efforts will make on other people. They want to know that they're not just throwing money down an endless pit that will never reach the people they're trying to help. They don't want to feel like their act of giving $100 will do absolutely nothing to remedy or solve the problem that you pointed out in step 1 of The Fundraising Funnel. Instead, donors want to be shown how their money will make an impact. Will it feed 10 more children? Will it save 100 puppies? What is it gonna DO.

First of all, this logical evaluation serves to make sure that a person isn't just wasting their money. You could have a credible cause, but if their money isn't going to help, then they don't want to join you on a sinking ship. When you demonstrate the impact their funds will have, they can wrap their head around making that donation. In addition, and more importantly, it serves to get their imagination working. When you state, as clear as day, that their money will give a family food for a month, then they can begin to imagine that family. They can start to think about how that family might feel, being fed for a month. It engages their active imagination, and the prospective donor starts to sell themselves on the idea of giving money.

The first step in the Holy Grail of Fundraising is to master this fundraising funnel. Without each step, you risk losing a potential donor's interest, commitment, or belief in your organization. When you streamline the funnel, you'll make sure there are no holes where potential donors "check out" and leave your marketing process. Equally important to the Fundraising Funnel is the Donor Pyramid, which I will cover next.

The Donor Pyramid

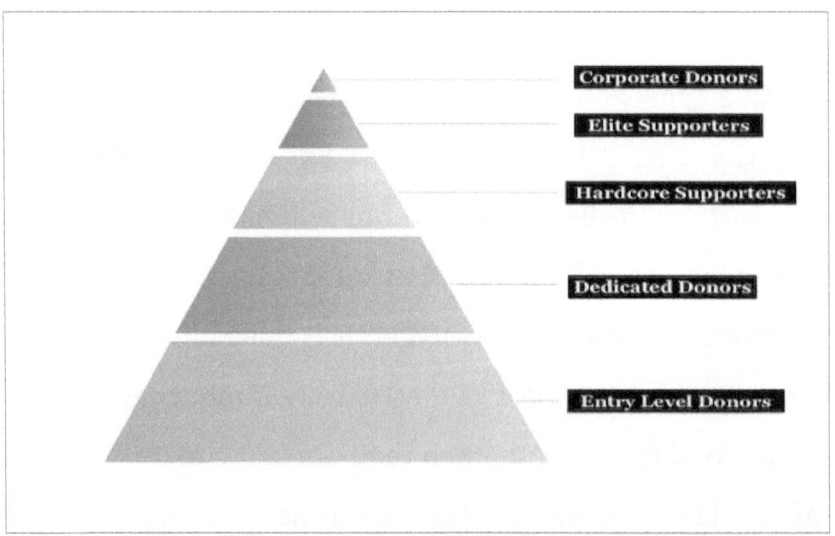

Simply put, the Donor Pyramid is the framework for your entire organization. By organizing your donor database this way, you'll be able to craft tailored marketing messages and set up a fundraising strategy for each level. For example, the communications that you send to your corporate donors should be very different than your entry level supporters. Right?

The bottom level of the pyramid is comprised of your first-time donors and those that give to your organization, but that aren't very engaged. These are people who trust you enough to give you money, but that aren't all that involved in your cause. It may just be a sympathy donation. They are also people who care about your cause, but not at the level where they're willing to engage yet in a larger way. But, thankfully, they *have* given money. This is the first step in the relationship-building process. It's your job to get them to move up the pyramid so that they can become a dedicated donor.

Did you know that *only 14%* of organizations prompt one-time donors to upgrade to a recurring gift during the donation process? This statistic was put out by NextAfter, and I think it's appalling. Especially because a simple popup that asks a one-time donor to upgrade results in a 64% increase in monthly donations! You're missing out on potential fundraising revenue if you don't encourage your one-time donors to become recurring donors. You're also doing the disservice of limiting the impact that individual can have on the world. Shame on you.

According to The State of Modern Philanthropy Report, the typical return donor makes a second donation around 349 days after their first donation. However, 19% of donors return within the first 90 days. In addition, one-time donors returned around 135 days sooner (4.5 months) to start a recurring gift, rather than to give a second one-time donation or become a fundraiser. Basically, people are *more interested in becoming a recurring donor* than to simply give another time to your nonprofit. One-time donors that upgrade to be a monthly donor will usually do this around 4 months.

If you're not trying to move your one-time donors from the "entry level donor" category to the "dedicated donor" category around month four, then you're missing out on a major opportunity. Wondering how much is a good monthly donation amount? Well, there's an answer for that too. According to the Blackbaud Luminate Online Report, monthly donors give $35.46 per month, or $425 a year. Rather than chasing down donors to give to your nonprofit, you can automate this all with a simple recurring monthly giving campaign.

After you have set up an automatic marketing campaign to transition entry level donors into being dedicated donors, then you can get to work on the next phase of the Donor Pyramid, which is hardcore supporters. I define these as individuals who are giving larger than average amounts to your organization, or those who are looking to devote their actual time to helping your nonprofit. This could take the form of volunteers. Your volunteers are supporters who believe in your mission so much that they are willing to devote their time and energy to helping you. They get to see the effects of your work first-hand, which emboldens their belief in your mission.

I think that nonprofits often times fall into two camps. The first is not believing that they can actually attract volunteers. The second is not paying enough attention to the volunteers they do have. They are separate problems. If you don't believe that there are people out there who want to make a difference by devoting their time, then you're sorely mistaken. According to NPSource 63 million Americans or 25% of the adult population volunteer their time, talents, and energy to making a difference. That's a heck of a lot of people! Also, 72% of volunteers are involved with only one organization, while 18.3% are involved with two. This means that these volunteers are people who believe in one mission, that of your organization.

It goes without saying that the volunteers are out there, you just have to ask them. If you notice that someone is highly engaged with your organization, why not offer them the opportunity to become a part of the team. The same study cited that 42% of people who volunteer did so as a result of being asked. If you're not asking, then you're missing out on people who can help your team… for free. What's even better is that you can automate this process as well, so that after a given amount of time (say 6 months) or after a certain number of donations, the person receives an invite to become a member of your volunteer staff.

On the flip side, I will also meet nonprofits who don't value their team. They don't appreciate them, send little thank you notes, or display any kind of gratitude. Since you're not paying them, you have to work extra hard to make sure your volunteers are at least getting something out of the process, in the way of enjoyment or a feeling of contributing to a larger purpose. On average, volunteers are worth about $24 per hour. You're saving a tremendous amount of money when you take on volunteers. You're avoiding having to pay people to help you with your initiatives. Thank them! Make sure that you assign someone who is in charge of this. It is a surefire way to bump up donor retention, along with creating more hardcore evangelists for your cause.

A certain portion of your donor database will be made up of elite supporters. As a new nonprofit, you might be able to count these on your hand, but that doesn't mean you shouldn't create a structured ask campaign for them. Elite supporters are typically high net worth individuals who believe in your cause. They are the ones giving thousands of dollars to your organization, or who are willing to sponsor a large project that you're doing. Likely, you are already being extraordinarily nice to these individuals, but where many organizations fall short is creating documents and content that capture the effect their having on their target audience.

Having a simple report of your efforts is great, but what if you took it a step further? What if you also created videos of your work in the field? What if you took the time to capture some stories of people you're helping in a well-worded blog post? Heck, you could even start a podcast to have real conversations with those elite donors, people you're helping, and to draw attention to your cause as a whole. There is the added bonus of being able to use all this extra content in your marketing materials.

Pay attention to what your elite supporters are looking to get out of their participation in your cause. This isn't always plainly stated. Sometimes, they like the feeling of impacting the world. Other times, they want to feel special and like the acclaim. Other times, they may get a kick out of interacting with your volunteers at the events you throw. They could even want to be on your board of directors. Pay attention, so that you can give them more of what they want and make sure they remain a lifelong elite donor.

Lastly, there are corporate donors, which make up the very sizable portion of donations to nonprofits in general. Entities, like Foundations and other organizations, could also fall into this category. The approach to attracting corporate donors is a bit different from individual givers. You must also treat them differently.

Remember, while a corporation is made up of individuals, its core purpose is to make a profit. Giving money to charity is a wise choice for a corporation because it improves its public image. It makes your donors view the corporation more positively. It also positively affects the corporation's customers.

A corporation wants to see that their funds have a positive effect, but they also want that result to be in-line with the values, vision, and mission of the corporation. The more that you can help a corporation have this experience, the more likely they will be to want to partner with your organization.

We've established that you need to master the Fundraising Funnel and the Donor Pyramid to really create a long-lasting nonprofit organization. Not only that but gaining confidence in these areas will also make sure you don't waste any opportunities to build and grow your organization.

There is only one thing that's missing in this epic quest for the holy grail… and that's a leader. If there is no leader, then this all falls apart. If no one is willing to step up and say "I will lead you on this quest," then a journey doesn't happen. And, that's your role in this process.

Let me get this straight. You can outsource marketing. You can have your staff manage the day to day of a nonprofit organization. You can even have a "spokesperson" who is the face of the cause. You can shine a light on the actual people you're helping, your volunteers, or your even your elite donors. But… you can't outsource leadership. It's all on you.

Being willing to step up and lead the charge is no easy feat. It requires dedication, enthusiasm, and a sense of mission. You can't look to anyone else for "the plan." It's your job to come up with that, along with the path forward for your organization. Heavy lies the crown, as they say. Thankfully, leadership is teachable. It will actually unlock a power within yourself that you might have never known was there. It will free up your time, make your nonprofit self-sustaining, and allow you to build powerful teams that lead the charge towards a better tomorrow.

In sales, the person with the most "certainty" will always convince the other person, no matter what the context of the scenario. By certainty, I'm referring to that inborn feeling of conviction, assertiveness, and confidence that is the hallmark of anyone who knows what they're doing and where they're going. Only, it's not enough to be simply certain of a belief or an opinion, you must also have the right materials to back it up. This forms the foundation of the promises that you make to your team, your board, your volunteers, and your staff. It's what you use to persuade others to join your cause.

You could do everything right that we talked about in the Donor Pyramid and the Fundraising Funnel, but if you, as the leader, aren't completely certain of your mission, then your followers will begin to have doubts. That lack of confidence may manifest in your voice, body language, written communications, or the way that talk about your cause. You must be 100% convinced that not only does your cause *deserve* attention, but that your efforts **WILL** have an impact on those who are in need.

We touched on this a bit when we covered your nonprofit story and the vision for your organization. Your **why** is at the heart of your mission, and your **how** will set your followers at ease. They will be able to relax, knowing that they are following a leader with a plan.

Think back to the last time you were in a situation where no one had a plan. How did it make you feel? Uncertain? Lost? Anxious? Frustrated? Human beings like being led. We enjoy it when someone knows what we're doing. It makes it so we don't have to think so hard to figure out the next course of action. It allows us to relax and focus on our own job, because we don't have to worry about the future. Someone else is already handling that. Often times, I meet nonprofit owners who shy away from being a leader because they don't want to impose their will or tell others what to do. On the contrary, people are begging for you to lead them to a better tomorrow. They don't want to have to think for themselves. That's why they are volunteering or working at your organization. They don't want to build their own! They just want to participate, and hopefully change the world for the better.

In the beginning stages of your nonprofit journey, you will be playing both the role of the leader and the manager. You'll be communicating and reiterating the vision, empowering others, and also managing the nuts and bolts of your specific project. Both are equal vital to the success of your organization. As a manager of your team, you'll be setting the specific goals for a one-time project, like setting up a donor database. You'll have a clear sense of the talents you bring, those of your staff, and what resources, tools, or skill sets that you must seek outside of your organization. I find management to be about the details and leadership to be more about the big picture.

At the end of the day, it is your leadership skills that will determine whether or not people follow you and buy into your vision. However, it is your management skills that will determine whether or not you actually accomplish that vision. If you have difficulty on the management side, make sure to either take classes to improve those skills, or identify someone who can play a leading role in the projects that are critical to the survival of your nonprofit.

As a comparison, you can think of it as the process that you might go through when planning a big trip. One of your friends might talk at length excitedly about a beautiful location in Hawaii. That "leader" of your friend group gets everyone excited and onboard to go on this big trip around the country. However, it's really another friend or two that does most of the nuts and bolts planning. They're the ones that do more of the coordination, selecting of the hotel, and making sure that everyone's on the same page.

Both roles are important to have a good experience. Without the leader, you'd never take the trip, but without those other friends to manage the experience, it wouldn't be very fun at all. Leadership is emotional and uses big picture thinking to sell followers on the vision. Management is more logical, practical, and detail oriented. It's focused on getting the dream realized.

Unfortunately, sometimes we see organizations that have great leadership, but horrible management. We also see orgs that have killer people and management, but not an ounce of vision. You need both if you really want to impact the world. To get started, all you have to be willing to do is recognize this simple fact, and to embrace each of these roles. The voyage to become a leader will not only shape the future of your nonprofit, but it will also help you grow as a person. It can be extremely rewarding. Ultimately, it will give you the strength that you need in order to face some of the major challenges on this planet.

Chapter 7: Conclusion

The faster you're able to implement some of these strategies into your nonprofit, the sooner you will begin to get results. It all comes down to that one word… action. You gotta take action. It might be difficult, because change is hard, but you can bet that it will set you up for an amazing future, where you can impact even more people throughout the world.

I was giving a talk a little ways back and afterwards, I had someone come up to me, grinning ear to ear. She was a woman in her mid 40s who had just started her very first nonprofit organization. She shook my hand and introduced herself. I glanced at the spiral notebook placed under the nook of her one arm. It was crammed with scribbling and bullet points.

"It's such a breath of fresh air to hear you talk!" she said, smiling. "Everything in this industry is so stuffy and boring. I love the passion you bring to this."

I thought a lot about that moment on my way back home. So much of learning a subject comes down to finding the right teachers. People who can show you the surest path to success, but who also bring a bit of spunk to their work. People who care more than others.

I hope that I've given you some great tricks, tips, and resources that you can apply to your nonprofit fundraising efforts. I also hope you enjoyed the process of learning some of these marketing hacks. Hopefully, in the coming years, they will become a part of the mainstream, rather than something that's reserved for for-profit companies and larger organizations.

I commend you for being willing to incorporate new strategies into your nonprofit. I can't wait for you to email me, raving about all of your newfound success. I wish nothing but the best for you, your organization, and those you are helping.

Good luck on your journey!

- Sal

P.S. If you enjoyed this book, please take a second to leave me a positive review on Amazon! Thanks!

About the Author

Salvador Briggman founded the popular blog, CrowdCrux, which has been cited by the New York Times, The Wallstreet Journal, CNN, and more. He helps entrepreneurs raise money on crowdfunding platforms like Kickstarter and Indiegogo. Last year, he helped nearly 400,000 individuals raise money from the crowd through his website, products, newsletter, and forum.